# Jesus Shows Up?

Rodney M. Howard-Browne

**River Publishing**

Unless otherwise indicated, all scriptural references are from the *King James Version* of the Bible.

Scripture portions marked "Amp." are taken from *The Amplified Bible,* copyright© 1987 by the Zondervan Corporation.

*What Happens When Jesus Shows Up?*
ISBN 1-884662-06-4
Copyright © 1997 by Revival Ministries International

Published by River Publishing
Tampa, Florida

Distributed by Word and Spirit Publishing
P.O. Box 701403
Tulsa, Oklahoma 74170
wordandspiritpublishing.com

# What Happens When Jesus Shows Up?

Chapter One

# The Anointing of Good News

*The Spirit of the Lord is upon me, because he hath anointed me to preach the gospel to the poor; he hath sent me to heal the brokenhearted, to preach deliverance to the captives, and recovering of sight to the blind, to set at liberty them that are bruised, to preach the acceptable year of the Lord.*

Luke 4:18,19

This is the message Jesus preached, the message He declared all during His earthly ministry.

The Spirit of the Lord is upon ME; He hath anointed ME to preach the gospel, and the gospel is GOOD NEWS.

There are too many "bad news" preachers in the earth today. All they want to do is bring doom and gloom.

Some people seem to think they are Old Testament prophets called to rail out against sin, but thank God we're under a new covenant. The message of this new covenant is the same message that Jesus proclaimed: the Spirit of the Lord is upon ME and He hath anointed ME to preach the gospel, the good news.

The gospel is good news, my dear friends. Good news. Good news. Good news. I bring you good news! I bring you glad tidings. I bring you GOOD NEWS. IT'S GOOD NEWS! HALLELUJAH! I get happy just thinking about the good news.

We all know the world is full of bad news. You can turn on television network headline news and all you hear is bad news. The last thing you need is a preacher coming along bringing you more bad news. We need to hear the good news of the gospel, that Jesus still saves, Jesus still heals, Jesus still sets free, Jesus is coming again. Hallelujah! Hallelujah! That's the gospel.

The problem is that many people are confused. They have a little bit of the old covenant, a little bit of the new covenant, and they've made up their own covenant. Their own "covenant" is one that brings them under condemnation and into death and bondage one minute and the next minute sets them free. In their confusion they think God is blessing them one moment and the next moment that God is saying, "I'm going to kill you." They walk around waiting for God to beat them and hurt them for reasons known only to Him.

That's not the good news. The good news is the same as it was when Jesus walked the earth. Do you know why it's still the same? Because Jesus is still the same; Jesus has not changed!

People say, "Well, Jesus wouldn't have meetings like you're having. And Jesus wouldn't do what you do."

Well, what would Jesus do? The question I pose to you is "What happens when Jesus shows up?" What happens when Jesus walks in the door?

Chapter Two

# What Happens When Jesus Shows Up?

I want you to know that when Jesus walks in the door, the very atmosphere of the room changes. When Jesus walks in the door, sickness and death and poverty and the curse of hell go out the back door, saying, "It's time for us to leave."

When Jesus walks in the door, you will know that He is there. You can see His nature, His character, in Matthew, Mark, Luke and John. What happens when He shows up? Jesus answered that Himself.

*The thief cometh not, but for to steal, and to kill, and to destroy: I am come that they might have life, and that they might have it more abundantly.*

John 10:10

*He that committeth sin is of the devil; for the devil sinneth from the beginning. For this purpose the Son of God was manifested, that he might destroy the works of the devil.*

I John 3:8

*How God anointed Jesus of Nazareth with the Holy Ghost and with power: who went about doing GOOD, and healing all that were oppressed of the devil; for God was with him.*

Acts 10:38

I have good news for you: God is GOOD; Jesus is GOOD. God wants to bless you; Jesus wants to bless you! Someone might ask, "What's all this about joy in the meetings? **WHY** joy? What is the purpose? Don't you know it's the *Holy* Spirit, not the *joy* spirit?"

Joy is a *fruit* of the Spirit, although it is not the *only* fruit of the Spirit. When the *Holy Spirit* does His work in your life, you will have *all* the nine fruit of the Spirit in your life. Joy is noticeable, however, because it is very much an outward expression that others can see.

> *A glad heart makes a cheerful countenance, but by sorrow of heart the spirit is broken.*
>
> **Prov. 15:13 Amp.**

Someone wrote, "Brother Rodney, Jesus didn't jump up and down and do cartwheels, and run around the place."

Maybe Jesus didn't but everybody He touched DID. They went walking and leaping and praising God! Walking and leaping and praising God! Walking and leaping and praising God! Oh, hallelujah!

Another person said, "You don't have to get emotional." I'm telling you right now, when He touches you, you want to shout it from the rooftops. You want to shout it from the mountaintops. Glory to God.

If you truly experience an encounter with the living God and are not stirred in your heart all the way through to your *emotions–then* I question that you had a real touch. If you can have an emotional response to something other than the Lord, such as a spouse, a child, a sporting event, a great triumph, or a great tragedy–then it is logical that your emotions would respond to the love and power of God in your life. Emotions are not *all* bad. Some emotions which come out of your *carnal* nature, such as anger, bitterness, hatred and lust, should be controlled and eliminated by the power of God. But to express good emotions is normal and healthy.

> *And my language and my message were not set forth in persuasive (enticing and plausible) words of wisdom, but they were in demonstration of the [Holy] Spirit and power [a proof by the Spirit and power of God, operating on me and stirring in the minds of my hearers the most holy emotions and thus persuading them].*
>
> I Cor. 2:4 Amp.

# What happens when Jesus shows up?

*Jesus meets all our needs*

According to the gospel, when Jesus walks in the door, He meets your every need.

Critics have said, "Well, it doesn't really seem there's any purpose in what's happening in your meetings because nobody's life depends upon receiving some joy."

The problem is that people are always looking for some great significance to read into everything Jesus did, but His heart was simply to meet people's needs-whatever they might be-to show us that God has provided for us in every situation-whatever the need.

Jesus always brings good news. Good news! He walked into the wedding in Cana of Galilee and what did they need there? They had run out of wine.

His turning the water into wine at the wedding in Cana of Galilee was a miracle, to be sure, but it wasn't especially dramatic. Nobody was dead; nobody's life depended upon the miracle. He was just showing His glory ... manifesting His power. John 2: 11 says, *This beginning of miracles did Jesus in Cana of Galilee* (when He turned the water into wine) *and manifested forth His glory ...*

You ask, "What is Jesus doing in the meetings you conduct?" Quite simply, He's doing what He's always done; He's just showing forth His glory.

Jesus walked into that wedding feast and was pushed into that miracle by His mother. He turned the water into wine and that's the first miracle He did, dear friends. What does that tell me? What does that tell you? It tells us that He wants to bless you. God is interested in even the least things in your life, the smallest details of everyday life. He wants to take care of you; He wants to meet your every need.

## What happens when Jesus shows up?

*Jesus will calm your storm*

Let's look in on Jesus in the back of a boat, sleeping. (See Mark 4:31-45) He and His disciples are taking a cruise across the lake, but, alas, a storm arises and the waves roll and the winds howl. The disciples are afraid and they run back and awaken Jesus.

What happened when He showed up? He walked into the middle of that storm and He commanded, "Peace be still!"

I want you to know He still calms the storms in our lives. It doesn't matter what your storm looks like. It doesn't matter what you're facing in your life; Jesus still calms the storm for you. You might think, "Well, maybe He's sleeping in the back of the boat." Then why don't you just go lie down at the back of the boat with Him and sleep along with Him? As long as He's sleeping, you can rest, too. Oh, glory to God. Hallelujah! He'll calm the storm for you.

## What happens when Jesus shows up?

*Jesus will deliver you from devils*

After the storm just mentioned, He went over into the country of the Gadarenes where a man with an unclean spirit (Legion) met Him. (See Mark 5:1-6) The devils took one look at Him and said, "Oh, oh, we have to go; we can't stay here anymore. We have to leave; we have to leave. Where can we go? Oh, there's a bunch of swine; let's go into those swine." The devils know they can't stay around when Jesus walks in the door.

## What happens when Jesus shows up?

*Jesus forgives our sins*

He walked up to a man with palsy and said, "Your sins are forgiven you." (See Matt. 9:2-8) When Jesus shows up, it's the absolute opposite of when the Pharisees show up. When the Pharisees and the Sadducees and the wouldn't-sees and couldn't-sees show up, they bring rocks. When Jesus shows up, He forgives sin!

It's easy for Him to forgive sin and heal the sick; it's so easy for Him. It is His nature and His purpose to forgive.

## What happens when Jesus shows up?

*Jesus will heal us*

A little woman had been sick for 12 years with an issue of blood and had spent all that she had on medical doctors who were unable to help her. (See Mark 5:25-34) When she heard that Jesus was going to pass by she said, "If I can just touch the hem of His garment, I'm going to be made whole." As she touched the hem of His garment, the power, the anointing, the *dunamis* that was on the life and the ministry of Jesus flowed out of Him into her and she was made whole. He said to her, "Go in peace and be whole of thy plague."

When Jesus shows up, He'll heal you. I don't care what you're facing. You might have an incurable disease right now, a disease that has been diagnosed as terminal. I want you to know that Jesus still heals today. He's the same yesterday, today and forever. Hallelujah!

## What happens when Jesus shows up?

He walked up to a blind man and said, "Receive your sight." Do you realize that all we need in our churches, all we need in America, is for Jesus to show up? When He walks in the door, He is going to make a difference.

The problem is that some people are waiting for Prophet Doodad to show up; you're waiting for Evangelist Dingaling or Apostle Bucketmouth to come along. "Oh, if only he would come to our town; if only he would come and hold a crusade, it would be so wonderful." You don't need any man; you need Jesus Christ, the Son of the living God. Hallelujah!

## What happens when Jesus shows up?

### Jesus gives us power

He said to His disciples, *Behold, I give unto you power to tread on serpents and scorpions, and*

*over all the power of the enemy ... (Luke 10:19 ).*
Hallelujah! When Jesus shows up, He gives
you power and authority, the same power and
authority He walked in on the earth.

## What happens when Jesus shows up?

### Jesus provides food

He found a multitude of people who didn't
have anything to eat and He took a little boy's
lunch and multiplied it, then fed thousands
upon thousands with five loaves and two
fishes. (See Matt. 14:15-21) That's what
happens when Jesus shows up!

## What happens when Jesus shows up?

### Jesus shows mercy to sinners

He walked along and saw a man named
Zacchaeus sitting up in a tree and He said,
"Come down, Zacchaeus. Let's go to your
house." (See Luke 19:2-9) You might feel stuck
way up in a tree right now, but I want you to

know that Jesus will show up and say, "Come on down; let's go to your house." Hallelujah!

## What happens when Jesus shows up?

### *Jesus will raise us from the dead*

Jairus, one of the rulers of the synagogue, fell down in the dusty road at Jesus' feet and said, "My daughter is sick at home." (See Mark 5:22-24 and 38-43) Jesus immediately went with Jairus to his home and because He walked into that house, the young girl was raised from the dead. When Jesus shows up, He brings new life!

## What happens when Jesus shows up?

He found a funeral procession outside the city of Nain; He pulled the boy right up out of the coffin, and gave him back to his mother. (See Luke 7: 11-15) When Jesus shows up, He'll raise the dead! Hallelujah!

## What happens when Jesus shows up?

He came to the tomb where Lazarus had been dead for four days. Lazarus' sisters were grieving. "Master, if You'd come earlier, this would not have happened. He's dead now, and stinketh." What happens when He shows up? He said these words, "Roll away the stone." And then He said these words, "Lazarus, come forth!"

You might be right in the middle of a situation where you have no hope, where things you've been believing and trusting God for, look dead; they look like they're buried in the tomb, stinking. But I want you to know that the same Jesus that walked the shores of Galilee 2,000 years ago comes to you and says, "Roll away the stone!" He says, "Lazarus, come forth!" Hallelujah! He brings life!

It doesn't matter what your circumstances say, when Jesus comes on the scene, seemingly impossible situations can be turned around. Jesus is our Miracle Worker!

It doesn't matter what the devil says. It doesn't matter what other people say. When Jesus walks in the door, everything changes. When Jesus walks in the door, there's no more argument. There's no more question, for He is the ANSWER. How can there be a question remaining when He is the Answer?

When He walks in the door, there's no more loss of direction. How can there be a loss of direction when He is the WAY?

When He walks in the door, there are no more lies. How can there be lies when He is the TRUTH?

When He walks in the door, there's no more death. How can there be death when He is the LIFE?

## What happens when Jesus shows up?

What happens when you've been in your boat all night fishing, but catching nothing? You have fished and you have fished (and you know how to fish because you area fisherman by trade), but you have caught absolutely nothing. When Jesus shows up, what does He do? Jesus comes to you and gives you clear direction, "Cast your nets on the other side."

You might be a minister of the gospel and you've been fishing all night. You've been fishing for years in Podunk Hollow but you've caught no fish. Jesus comes to you now and says, "Cast your nets on the other side." Hallelujah!

Your first thought might be to say, "Brother Rodney, you can't be serious. Surely He won't meet every need ... not every single need. *Some* He will meet, yes ... but surely not *every* need."

YES, He will meet *every* need, *every* one. Some people think His power is only for a life-and death situation. But that's not true; in fact, Jesus used His power not only to touch people round about Him in every area of their lives, but to meet His own needs in His own ministry, as well.

When the disciples needed tax money, for instance, Jesus said to Peter, "Go down and catch the first fish. The money that you need is in his mouth."

When you have a need, I don't care how simple the need is, or how complicated, when Jesus shows up, He's going to meet that need. That is the gospel; that is the gospel; that is the gospel! GOOD NEWS!

## Jesus is our Miracle Worker!

Think about this for a moment: Jesus walked on water. Nobody benefited from that miracle except Him. You might say, "Why, then, did He walk on water?" He walked on water because He needed to get to the other side! I know why He walked on water: because He was in ministry and when you're in ministry, you need to get away from people *sometimes*. When Jesus walked on water, it did not seem like a necessity, but a luxury. He could have waited for a boat.

If the Pharisees had gotten hold of Jesus, they would have said, "You're abusing God's power; how dare you walk on water and use it for your own benefit? You need to walk normally on the ground like we all have to do. Who do You think You are, walking on the water? From now on, please refrain from walking on water and start walking on the ground. Look at You, taking God's power and using it for Yourself."

I believe that Jesus walked on water to show us that He had control over the elements as a sign and a wonder. But I also believe that He did it to show us that if we are obeying and serving God-then we can trust Him to make a way for us where there is no way. Most of the time we have no faith for the supernatural, but God wants us to know that His supernatural power is there for us when we need it.

*And Jesus looking upon them saith, With men it is impossible, but not with God: for with God all things are possible.*

**Mark 10:27**

## What happens when Jesus shows up?

When Jesus shows up, He says to you, "Be of good cheer." When Jesus shows up, He says, "Rejoice! Rejoice! Rejoice!" When Jesus shows up, He says, "Be strong."

## What happens when Jesus shows up?

*Jesus brings joy!*

Listen carefully: in the Book of Acts, chapter 8, we see that Philip went down to the city of Samaria and preached Christ to them and there was great joy in the city. What happens when Jesus shows up? There is great joy in the city when Jesus shows up. Hallelujah!

## What happens when Jesus shows up?

We could go on and on telling what happens when Jesus shows up. He showed up at the Pool of Bethesda, which had five porches, and in those five porches lay a great multitude of blind and halt and maimed and withered people. What happened when Jesus showed up? He walked in and found a man who had been there for a long time. He didn't have anybody to help him get into that pool but Jesus said, "Take up your bed and walk!" When Jesus shows up, He tells you, "Arise! Take up your bed and walk."

"Brother Rodney, you're too excited about this; you just need to calm down. You're just too excited about this. It can't be as good as what you're telling us."

Yes, I am excited about this, because it's real. If you want Jesus to show up at your house, you are going to have to break religion and tradition in your life. Religion and tradition make the gospel ineffective.

> *So for the sake of your tradition (the rules handed down by your forefathers), you have set aside the Word of God [depriving it of force and authority and making it of no effect].*

> **Matt. 15:6 Amp.**

When Jesus shows up, it's good news. It's good news. Good news! GOOD NEWS!

You say, "Brother Rodney, I would love for Jesus to show up in my house. I would love for Jesus to show up in my church. I would love for Jesus to show up in my town." The truth is, if you are born again, Jesus *will* show up when you do, because He's in you! He is in you! Greater is He that is in you than he that is in the world!

You're waiting for Jesus to show up and He's waiting for you to show up. He already *did* show up.

Jesus has done everything He can do to bring you everything you need. He is waiting for you to believe it, to receive it for your life, and to see it manifested. Jesus is here right now, visiting your house! Just receive your need met as it would have been if Jesus had come to your house during His earthly ministry. You have a *better* covenant. The only thing standing in your way is doubt and unbelief.

> *Jesus replied, Have I been with all of you for so long a time, and do you not recognize and know Me yet, Philip?*

*Anyone who has seen Me has seen the Father. How can you say then, Show us the Father? Do you not believe that I am in the Father, and that the Father is in Me? What I am telling you I do not say on My own authority and of My own accord; but the Father Who lives continually in Me does the (His) works (His own miracles, deeds of power).*

*Believe Me that I am in the Father and the Father in Me; or else believe Me for the sake of the [very] works themselves. [If you cannot trust Me, at least let these works that I do in My Father's name convince you.] I assure you, most solemnly I tell you, if anyone steadfastly believes in Me, he will himself be able to do the things that I do; and he will do even greater things than these, because I go to the Father.*

John 14:9-12 Amp.

If Jesus lives in us, we can do the same things that He did. He even said *greater* works we would do. All we have to do is to take Him at His Word and BELIEVE IT!

For information regarding books, audio tapes, and video tapes, please write to us at the address below:

Revival Ministries International
P.O. Box 292888
Tampa FL 33687 • USA

Dr. Rodney Howard-Browne, and his wife, Adonica, are the founders of Revival Ministries International, The River at Tampa Bay Church, and River Bible Institutes in Tampa, Florida. They, and their ministry team, travel about 46 weeks of the year, holding weekly meetings in cities across North America and also to sixty nations of the world. Their commission is to win the lost, and to awaken the Church to fulfill the Great Commission. Drs. Rodney and Adonica founded The River at Tampa Bay Church on December 1, 1996 – a multi-racial church, representing a cross-section of society from rich to poor, from all nations, bringing people to a place of maturity in their Christian walk. The River Bible Institutes, founded in 1997, consist of the River Bible Institute, River School of Worship, River School of Government, River School of Church Planting, and River Bible Institute Español. For more information about Dr. Rodney Howard-Browne, R.M.I., The River at Tampa Bay Church, and R.B.I., please, visit revival.com.